Ivy Global

MW00620911

SSAT & ISEE

VOCABULARY 1, EDITION 2.0

MADE WITH CARE

NEW YORK

This publication was written and edited by the team at Ivy Global.

Editors: Sacha Azor and Natalia Irizarry-Cole

Producers: Lloyd Min and Junho Suh

Developers: Alexandra Candib, Lei Huang, Amelia McLeod, Yolanda Song, and Adam Wolsky

About Ivy Global

Ivy Global is a pioneering education company that produces high-quality educational material.

E-mail: publishing@ivyglobal.com
Website: http://www.ivyglobal.com

Introduction

Welcome, students and parents! This pocketbook is intended to help students prepare for the level of vocabulary encountered on the SSAT & ISEE. For students applying to many top private and independent schools in North America, these exams are a crucial and sometimes daunting step in the admissions process. By helping you master these core vocabulary words, Ivy Global will help you build your confidence and maximize your score on these important exams.

Comprehensive Prep

We know that no two students are exactly alike—each student brings unique personal strengths to his or her test preparation. For this reason, we've tailored our preparation materials to help students with a specific subject area or goal. Ivy Global also offers full sets of SSAT and ISEE books to help students develop the best strategies for each section of these exams:

- *SSAT English, SSAT Math, SSAT Practice*
- *ISEE English, ISEE Math, ISEE Practice*

This book is the first in a set of three vocabulary pocketbooks for the SSAT and ISEE that include a total of 365 words for every-day learning:

- *Vocabulary 1* (Essential) – Words 1-125
- *Vocabulary 2* (Extended) – Words 126-250
- *Vocabulary 3* (Advanced) – Words 251-365

Ivy Global's products are available for purchase at ivyglobal.com/products or amazon.com.

How to Use This Book

This book is a study aid; it isn't a complete dictionary. The words here are selected because they are likely to be useful when studying for the SSAT and ISEE, and we've given brief definitions to help you quickly learn the most common meaning of each word. There is more information available about each word, including information about less common definitions and the history and etymology of each word.

- When you learn a word, pay attention to its part of speech (is it a noun, verb, adjective, or adverb?) and look for other possible definitions of the word.
- Be sure to write your own personal sentence for each word to help you remember it.
- When you're writing your sentence, if you don't totally understand the meaning of a word you should try to search for other sentences containing the word.
- Use a pencil, and have a trusted reader check your sentences.
- Correct your sentences if you don't quite capture the meanings of the words on your first try.
- In order to master as many words as possible before your exam, create a daily schedule and make sure to review old words while you are learning new ones.

Sample Study Schedule

To begin, try using this sample study plan as a model for your own personalized study schedule.

Sample Study Schedule		
Week	Words this Week	Goal Reached?
1	1 - 25	☐
2	26 - 50	☐
3	51 - 75	☐
4	76 - 100	☐
5	101 – 125	☐
6	Final Review	☐

We recommend focusing on 10-40 words each week. The table above is for a schedule of learning 25 words per week.

Learning New Words

As you work through these vocabulary words, make sure that you're using the most effective strategies.

Use mnemonics: Mnemonics are devices to help improve your memory and can be used to help you remember difficult words. They can use combinations of words, images, patterns of letters or a myriad of other things. Mnemonic devices should only be used with words that are complex—short, easy to remember words can actually become more complicated with the use of a mnemonic device. Mnemonics help you convert abstract information into a mix of what you already know.

You can use similar sounding words to remember a new one:

- There are no sirens in this serene neighborhood.

Siren is something that is loud and annoying, but serene means "calm and clear." A lack of sirens will make for a serene environment.

- The wrecking ball was raised to raze the building.

Raze means "destroy," and a wrecking ball would probably get the job done.

You can also use something more visual:

- Novel tea would be a novelty. Usually tea is made from plants, not books!

Expand your classroom: Don't think of learning vocabulary as something you need to do just for the SSAT or ISEE. Instead, try to make these words a part of your everyday life. There are lots of creative ways you can use your new vocabulary words:

- Start using the words you learn in essays and homework assignments.
- Try making a tricky word your theme for an art project.
- Use new words in conversations with friends and family.
- Tape flash cards or put sticky notes with the words you're learning around your house and recite the definition of a word each time you see it.
- Compete with your friends to see who can master the most words.
- Draw a picture that captures the meaning of a word.

Know Connotations: A word's connotation is its secondary meaning, or the feeling we get from the word. A word can have a positive (+) connotation if it means something good, a negative (-) connotation if it means something bad, or a neutral connotation if it is neither good nor bad.

For example, the word "horrible" has a negative connotation, whereas "joyous" has a positive connotation. If you can remember that a word means something positive or negative, you may be able to eliminate answer choices with the opposite connotation if you encounter them on your exam.

Come up with contexts: If you want to remember multiple definitions of a word, one useful strategy is to come up with many contexts—phrases where you might have heard the word before. A word's context is everything in a phrase or sentence that might influence the word's meaning. The word "charge," for example can have many different meanings, depending on its context. It might be helpful to make yourself a bubble chart and think of as many phrases as you can:

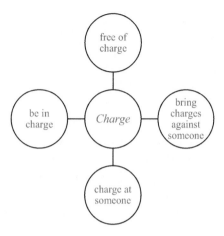

What does "charge" mean in each of these contexts? "Free of charge" means that you don't have to pay for something; to "be in charge" means to have power or be in control; to "charge at someone" means to attack suddenly or assault; and to "bring charges against someone" means to accuse or blame.

Let's begin!

adequate

sufficient; acceptable (adj)

Her parents didn't mind that she wasn't making straight A's as long as her grades were adequate.

Your sentence:

_____

_____

_____

_____

_____

_____

adorn

decorate (v)

He adorned his room with posters of his favorite movies.

Your sentence:

_____

_____

_____

_____

_____

_____

adversity

misfortune; challenging circumstances (n)

Her childhood was too full of adversity for her to remember it fondly.

Your sentence:

_____

_____

_____

_____

_____

_____

aesthetic

relating to art or beauty (adj)

Those shoes are certainly comfortable, but they have little aesthetic value.

Your sentence:

_____

_____

_____

_____

_____

_____

aggravate

annoy; make worse (v)

The students' fondness for passing notes in class aggravated their teacher.

Your sentence:

_____

_____

_____

_____

_____

_____

alleviate

make less severe (v)

My favorite ways to alleviate stress are listening to upbeat music and spending time with friends.

Your sentence:

_____

_____

_____

_____

_____

_____

amateur

nonprofessional;
unskilled (adj)

Her pictures are so well-composed that it's hard
to believe she's an amateur photographer.

Your sentence:

_____

_____

_____

_____

_____

_____

ambiance

the atmosphere or mood of a place (n)

The string quartet and candlelit tables gave the restaurant a luxurious ambiance.

Your sentence:

_____

_____

_____

_____

_____

_____

ambiguous

unclear; uncertain (adj)

The Mona Lisa's ambiguous smile gives the painting a sense of mystery.

Your sentence:

_____

_____

_____

_____

_____

_____

animosity

intense hostility (n)

The animosity between the director and the lead actor made rehearsals an unpleasant experience for the rest of the cast.

Your sentence:

_____

_____

_____

_____

_____

_____

anomaly

something abnormal (n)

An anomaly in the results of her blood test revealed that she had a serious medical condition.

Your sentence:

_____

_____

_____

_____

_____

_____

arid

dry; barren (adj)

The desert is so arid that only cacti can survive.

Your sentence:

_____

_____

_____

_____

_____

_____

articulate

able to speak fluently and logically (adj); express precisely (v)

The college professor was surprised by how articulate the high school student was.

Your sentence:

_____

_____

_____

_____

_____

_____

authentic

genuine (adj)

An authentic designer bag is much more expensive than a knock-off you can buy on the street.

Your sentence:

_____

_____

_____

_____

_____

_____

bemuse

confuse,
bewilder (v)

The detective was bemused by the evidence that seemed to point at two different suspects for the same crime.

Your sentence:

_____

_____

_____

_____

_____

_____

bewilder

confuse severely (v)

At first she was bewildered by Shakespeare's old-fashioned language, but after using a modern translator he became one of her favorite authors.

Your sentence:

_____

_____

_____

_____

_____

_____

blend

mix together (v); a mixture of multiple things (n)

The trick to a good sauce is to make sure you blend the ingredients completely.

Your sentence:

_____

_____

_____

_____

_____

_____

bliss

total happiness (n)

A cozy chair and a good book is my vision of bliss.

Your sentence:

_____

_____

_____

_____

_____

_____

boisterous

energetic; noisy (adj)

We could hear his boisterous laughter all the way across the room.

Your sentence:

_____

_____

_____

_____

_____

_____

brandish

wave something in anger or excitement (v)

She brandished her sword to show the king that she was serious about leading the army.

Your sentence:

_____

_____

_____

_____

_____

_____

capitulate

surrender; to give in (v)

She pouted and whined and begged, but her parents would not capitulate to her demands for her own car.

Your sentence:

_____

_____

_____

_____

_____

_____

chasm

a deep divide (n)

Over time, water can turn a small dent on the surface of the earth into a chasm hundreds of feet deep.

Your sentence:

_____

_____

_____

_____

_____

_____

chronological

in the order in which events occurred (adj)

This summer, she plans to read every book by Toni Morrison in chronological order according to when they were published.

Your sentence:

_____

_____

_____

_____

_____

_____

circumvent

find a way around (v)

If we stick to the trail on the map, we'll circumvent any seriously dangerous terrain.

Your sentence:

_____

_____

_____

_____

_____

_____

collaborate

work together (v)

Although I don't mind working alone, I think it's more fun to collaborate with others.

Your sentence:

_____

_____

_____

_____

_____

_____

colleague

someone a person works with in the same organization or profession (n)

The job itself was a little boring, but her friendly colleagues made it more interesting.

Your sentence:

_____

_____

_____

_____

_____

_____

comprehend

understand (v)

Kelsey couldn't comprehend why her little brother liked putting ketchup on his peas.

Your sentence:

_____

_____

_____

_____

_____

_____

conjecture

idea or opinion
without evidence (n)

The notion that the medicine could lead to
trouble sleeping was based on conjecture and
needed to be proven in a clinical trial.

Your sentence:

_____

_____

_____

_____

_____

_____

conservative

traditional; cautious (adj)

His conservative style of dressing was uncommon at the high school, which had no dress code restrictions.

Your sentence:

_____

_____

_____

_____

_____

_____

contend

argue; assert (v)

Leticia contended that she was the best choice for the assignment, despite her inexperience.

Your sentence:

_____

_____

_____

_____

_____

_____

courtesy

respect, politeness (n)

Although disappointed that she did not accept the job offer, the manager was pleased that Jessica had the courtesy to tell him that she had taken another job.

Your sentence:

_____

_____

_____

_____

_____

_____

creed

Ivy Global

system of beliefs (n)

United States law allows all men and women to practice their creed freely.

Your sentence:

_____

_____

_____

_____

_____

_____

custom

traditional behavior (n)

It is a common custom for Europeans to have long meals with their families.

Your sentence:

_____

_____

_____

_____

_____

_____

dearth

lack (n)

People constantly called and emailed to ask questions about the company because of the dearth of information on their website.

Your sentence:

_____

_____

_____

_____

_____

_____

debacle

disaster (n)

The decision to hire inexperienced staff proved to be a major debacle for the restaurant during its peak season.

Your sentence:

_____

_____

_____

_____

_____

_____

deduct

take away; subtract (v)

The manager deducted $500 off the employee's paycheck after she arrived late every day for a month.

Your sentence:

_____

_____

_____

_____

_____

_____

defective

not functioning (adj)

Joseph returned the defective computer to the store, and the company replaced it with a new one.

Your sentence:

_____

_____

_____

_____

_____

_____

delight

please (v); pleasure (n)

It delighted Norah to hear that her best friend Sandra would be visiting Philadelphia.

Your sentence:

_____

_____

_____

_____

_____

_____

demolish

destroy (v)

The construction crew demolished the old mansion in order to begin construction on the new apartment building.

Your sentence:

_____

_____

_____

_____

_____

_____

deteriorate

fall apart (v)

Without anyone to maintain it, the abandoned warehouse deteriorated quickly.

Your sentence:

_____

_____

_____

_____

_____

_____

disperse

scatter (v)

The group of antelopes dispersed after they saw the lion pack approaching.

Your sentence:

_____

_____

_____

_____

_____

_____

durable

long-lasting (adj)

Although the sports car was more attractive, George decided to buy the durable sedan, which he knew would be more reliable in the end.

Your sentence:

_____

_____

_____

_____

_____

_____

efface

erase (v)

The rain effaced the criminal's footsteps, leaving us with no trail to follow.

Your sentence:

_____

_____

_____

_____

_____

_____

elation

intense joy (n)

When the numbers read by the TV host matched Miguel's lottery ticket, he felt an elation he had never before experienced.

Your sentence:

_____

_____

_____

_____

_____

_____

embrace

accept enthusiastically (v)

Exhausted from studying for four consecutive hours, Jillian embraced the idea of taking a break.

Your sentence:

_____

_____

_____

_____

_____

_____

enigma

Ivy Global

puzzle (n)

The disappearance of Nancy's wallet remained an enigma to her; she clearly remembered taking it with her to work.

Your sentence:

_____

_____

_____

_____

_____

_____

erratic

unpredictable (adj)

New York's erratic weather can make it difficult to know what to wear in the morning.

Your sentence:

_____

_____

_____

_____

_____

_____

evade

avoid (v)

Derek evaded washing the dishes in the morning by pretending he was late to work.

Your sentence:

_____

_____

_____

_____

_____

_____

exalt

praise (v)

After successfully landing on the moon, Neil
Armstrong was exalted as a hero.

Your sentence:

_____

_____

_____

_____

_____

_____

exonerate

remove guilt or blame (v)

The defendant was exonerated after the DNA tests proved her innocence.

Your sentence:

_____

_____

_____

_____

_____

_____

expel

remove by force (v)

The student was expelled from the school after he was caught cheating on an exam.

Your sentence:

_____

_____

_____

_____

_____

_____

extravagant

unnecessarily fancy (adj)

When David and Veronica walked into the
Johnsons' house, they found the diamond
chandelier too extravagant for their taste.

Your sentence:

_____

_____

_____

_____

_____

_____

feeble

weak; inadequate (adj)

His feeble excuse for missing class landed him in detention.

Your sentence:

_____

_____

_____

_____

_____

_____

ferocity

fierceness (n)

We were in awe of the mother bear's ferocity in defending her cubs.

Your sentence:

_____

_____

_____

_____

_____

_____

fiasco

Ivy Global

failure, disaster, farce (n)

We had high hopes for our latest business venture, but it turned out to be a financial fiasco.

Your sentence:

_____

_____

_____

_____

_____

_____

flamboyant

attention-grabbing (adj)

As the oft-ignored middle child, she frequently resorted to flamboyant clothing to attract the attention she craved.

Your sentence:

_____

_____

_____

_____

_____

_____

gaffe

an embarrassing
mistake (n)

The actor's gaffe was on tabloid front pages for a week.

Your sentence:

_____

_____

_____

_____

_____

_____

glitch

minor malfunction (n)

A computer glitch meant that I couldn't save my work, so I had to rewrite the last page of my assignment.

Your sentence:

_____

_____

_____

_____

_____

_____

hoax

trick, deception, con (n);
trick, deceive, con (v)

Watch out for hoaxes on April Fools' Day.

Your sentence:

_____

_____

_____

_____

_____

_____

idiosyncrasy

eccentricity, quirk (n)

When writing, remember that a few idiosyncrasies can make a boring character more likeable.

Your sentence:

_____

_____

_____

_____

_____

_____

impeccable

faultless, perfect (adj)

As a teenager, he was well-liked by his friends' parents because of his impeccable manners.

Your sentence:

_____

_____

_____

_____

_____

_____

impertinent

irrelevant; insolent, disrespectful (adj)

The high school teacher was becoming tired of the impertinent comments her students often made.

Your sentence:

_____

_____

_____

_____

_____

_____

innovation

a novel idea or thing (n)

Her most recent innovation increased productivity in the office by more than fifty percent.

Your sentence:

_____

_____

_____

_____

_____

_____

instigate

initiate; provoke (v)

His hot temper and strong opinions often instigated heated arguments.

Your sentence:

_____

_____

_____

_____

_____

_____

investigate

thoroughly examine (v)

We cannot form conclusions until we have investigated the claims.

Your sentence:

_____

_____

_____

_____

_____

_____

ironic

different from what is expected; sarcastic (adj)

It was ironic that the concoction he took every day for his symptoms was actually making them worse.

Your sentence:

_____

_____

_____

_____

_____

_____

laborious

labor-intensive, arduous, effortful (adj)

Olympic athletes must undertake years of laborious training.

Your sentence:

_____

_____

_____

_____

_____

_____

laud

praise (v)

This article should laud her achievements in mathematics, not criticize her appearance.

Your sentence:

_____

_____

_____

_____

_____

_____

livid

furious (adj)

The news that her social services were being cut yet again left her livid.

Your sentence:

_____

_____

_____

_____

_____

_____

lore

mythology, stories, body of traditions or knowledge (n)

The myth of the haunted house on Pecan Street is a large part of our town's lore.

Your sentence:

_____

_____

_____

_____

_____

_____

loquacious

talkative (adj)

She was so loquacious and charming that there was never an awkward silence with her.

Your sentence:

_____

_____

_____

_____

_____

_____

malice

ill will, spite (n)

The musician's ex-boyfriend did not give a fair evaluation of her performance; instead, his review was motivated by malice.

Your sentence:

_____

_____

_____

_____

_____

_____

medley

Ivy Global

assortment, mixture, miscellany (n)

The children at the party have very different food preferences, so the parent bought a medley of snacks for them to share.

Your sentence:

_____

_____

_____

_____

_____

_____

merit

worthiness, value (n); deserve, warrant (v)

The debators should be judged not on their charm or confidence, but on the merits of their arguments.

Your sentence:

_____

_____

_____

_____

_____

_____

mock

make fun of (v)

Jessica would often mock her brother's short stature.

Your sentence:

_____

_____

_____

_____

_____

_____

modify

alter; change (v)

After students began dropping her class, Professor Smith modified her curriculum to entice them to stay.

Your sentence:

_____

_____

_____

_____

_____

_____

narrative

story (n)

The police became skeptical when listening to Aaron's inconsistent narrative.

Your sentence:

_____

_____

_____

_____

_____

_____

nemesis

enemy (n)

After his army lost the battle, David swore he would defeat his nemesis the next time.

Your sentence:

_____

_____

_____

_____

_____

_____

nimble

quick; agile (adj)

The soccer player's nimble moves helped her team to victory.

Your sentence:

_____

_____

_____

_____

_____

_____

obsolete

no longer current (adj)

CD players are obsolete; people prefer to listen to music on their computers instead.

Your sentence:

_____

_____

_____

_____

_____

_____

obstinate

stubborn (adj)

The obstinate boy would not follow
instructions, even after being told several times.

Your sentence:

_____

_____

_____

_____

_____

_____

opponent

person or group competing against another (n)

Manuela and her opponent Jeffrey were nearly evenly matched in the chess game.

Your sentence:

_____

_____

_____

_____

_____

_____

overt

obvious (adj)

She liked people who didn't try to hide their intentions, so she found his overt flirtation charming.

Your sentence:

_____

_____

_____

_____

_____

_____

pact

agreement (n)

After William broke Jordan's lamp, the brothers made a pact not to play catch in the house again.

Your sentence:

_____

_____

_____

_____

_____

_____

painstaking

difficult; with great effort (adj)

Patricia's painstaking attention to detail led to the capture of the criminal, as well as a promotion to detective.

Your sentence:

_____

_____

_____

_____

_____

_____

paradox

something that does not follow (n)

It seemed like a paradox to Matilda: it was raining, but the sun was shining brightly.

Your sentence:

_____

_____

_____

_____

_____

_____

peril

danger (n)

Alexandra knew she was in peril when she could not find her way out of the lion's den.

Your sentence:

_____

_____

_____

_____

_____

_____

pester

annoy (v)

Timothy would constantly pester his sister by standing in front of the TV while she was watching her favorite show.

Your sentence:

_____

_____

_____

_____

_____

_____

practical

useful, logical (adj)

The book, marketed as a language guide for travel, was not very practical, as it did not include information about hotels or airports.

Your sentence:

_____

_____

_____

_____

_____

_____

precocious

advanced at a young age (adj)

The precocious child could speak three languages fluently by the time she turned seven.

Your sentence:

_____

_____

_____

_____

_____

_____

preserve

maintain (v)

To preserve the freshness of those berries, you should put them in the refrigerator.

Your sentence:

_____

_____

_____

_____

_____

_____

prominent

well-known, important (adj)

Rebecca was excited to introduce her friends to the prominent guest at her party.

Your sentence:

_____

_____

_____

_____

_____

_____

prototype

original model (n)

The prototype of the computer was incredibly fast, but needed to be altered.

Your sentence:

_____

_____

_____

_____

_____

_____

query

question, request (n)

The parents had various queries for the teacher after their children came home confused from the lesson.

Your sentence:

_____

_____

_____

_____

_____

_____

rapid

fast (adj)

The cheetah is perhaps the most rapid land animal, running as fast as 70 miles per hour for short distances.

Your sentence:

_____

_____

_____

_____

_____

_____

raze

destroy (v)

The historic mansion was razed in order to make room for a new office building in one of the city's oldest neighborhoods.

Your sentence:

_____

_____

_____

_____

_____

_____

redundant

extra, unnecessary, duplicated (adj)

Her first explanation was useful, but her attempts to clarify it were just redundant.

Your sentence:

_____

_____

_____

_____

_____

_____

remedy

cure (n)

There is no known remedy to the common cold, but rest and vitamin C are said to speed up the recovery.

Your sentence:

_____

_____

_____

_____

_____

_____

reprimand

criticize, condemn (v)

After the child was caught stealing candy, he was severely reprimanded by his parents.

Your sentence:

_____

_____

_____

_____

_____

_____

retort

respond in a forceful manner (v)

After hearing Pete's position on the issue, Jane retorted with a stern critique.

Your sentence:

_____

_____

_____

_____

_____

_____

rural

characteristic of the countryside (adj)

John's cottage was located in a rural area, surrounded by fields and forests.

Your sentence:

_____

_____

_____

_____

_____

_____

sage

wise individual (n)

The sage's poignant answer to my question about the meaning of life came from his many years of knowledge and wisdom.

Your sentence:

_____

_____

_____

_____

_____

_____

sarcastic

ironically mocking (adj)

He was being sarcastic when he told his mom that the burnt cookies she had made looked appetizing.

Your sentence:

_____

_____

_____

_____

_____

_____

scoff

mock or ridicule (v)

When her mother told her to turn off the TV and do her homework, Jessica scoffed and said that watching the show was her homework for acting class.

Your sentence:

_____

_____

_____

_____

_____

secure

safe from harm; firmly attached (adj)

When Juan was a young boy he was afraid of the dark, but his teddy bear always made him feel secure.

Your sentence:

_____

_____

_____

_____

_____

_____

serene

completely calm; clear (adj)

Angie felt serene as she meditated next to a quiet mountain stream, far away from the city.

Your sentence:

_____

_____

_____

_____

_____

_____

skeptic

someone who doubts (n)

Naoko was a well-known skeptic because she never trusted the articles in the newspaper.

Your sentence:

_____

_____

_____

_____

_____

_____

sloth

inactivity, laziness (n)

The cold weather inclined her towards sloth, so she skipped her usual jog.

Your sentence:

_____

_____

_____

_____

_____

_____

sly

sneaky or mischievous (adj)

She took a sly bite of cake, knowing that she wasn't supposed to eat dessert before dinner.

Your sentence:

_____

_____

_____

_____

_____

_____

sporadic

occurring at irregular intervals (adj)

The rainfall in the desert was sporadic, only occuring a few times per year.

Your sentence:

_____

_____

_____

_____

_____

_____

stifle

suppress or stop (v)

She didn't want to disrupt the minute of silence, so she made her best effort to stifle her cough.

Your sentence:

_____

_____

_____

_____

_____

_____

subtle

difficult to notice
or describe (adj)

There were only subtle differences between the identical twins.

Your sentence:

_____

_____

_____

_____

_____

_____

sympathize

feel sorry for (v)

It was not difficult to sympathize with the flood victims.

Your sentence:

_____

_____

_____

_____

_____

_____

tact

the ability to act or speak without offending others (n)

He presented his argument with such tact that both sides agreed with him.

Your sentence:

_____

_____

_____

_____

_____

_____

tentative

not certain (adj)

He made tentative plans with Jessica, hoping that he would get the day off of work.

Your sentence:

_____

_____

_____

_____

_____

_____

timid

shy (adj)

He was very timid in approaching his teacher for an extension on his homework because he was worried she wouldn't give him one.

Your sentence:

_____

_____

_____

_____

_____

_____

tolerance

open-mindedness;
endurance (n)

The bacteria have a high tolerance for variations in temperature.

Your sentence:

_____

_____

_____

_____

_____

_____

unconventional

out of the ordinary (adj)

She was sad to dye her pink hair back to black, but her new boss frowned on unconventional hair colors.

Your sentence:

_____

_____

_____

_____

_____

_____

uniform

the same (adj)

Every window in the apartment is a uniform width.

Your sentence:

_____

_____

_____

_____

_____

_____

universal

the same for all cases (adj)

It is considered a universal rule at the school that all students must wear black shoes.

Your sentence:

_____

_____

_____

_____

_____

_____

vendetta

grudge (n)

The Smith family had a vendetta against the Jones family because of a land dispute between their great grandparents.

Your sentence:

_____

_____

_____

_____

_____

_____

vital

extremely important; energetic (adj)

Protecting our rivers and oceans is essential because water is such a vital resource.

Your sentence:

_____

_____

_____

_____

_____

_____

vivid

powerful, clear (adj)

Her dream was so vivid it felt real.

Your sentence:

_____

_____

_____

_____

_____

_____

vulnerable

open to attack or harm (adj)

In self-defense classes you learn to shield your neck, which is one of the most vulnerable parts of the body.

Your sentence:

_____

_____

_____

_____

_____

_____

wicked

Ivy Global

evil or wrong (adj)

The wicked witch cast spells on everyone she didn't like.

Your sentence:

_____

_____

_____

_____

_____

_____

Made in the USA
Middletown, DE
05 September 2023